Elise

Versailles
dates and figures

Several books on the Palace of Versailles have been published, however none of them have yet treated succinctly the questions, usually very simple, that many visitors and tourists ask themselves after a first visit. In order to answer the most frequent questions, the main dates that made the history of Versailles have been gathered, as well as several figures concerning the buildings, the gardens or simply the people who have been involved in its history.

EDITIONS JEAN-PAUL GISSEROT
www.editions-gisserot.com

Versailles in 104 Dates...

The Palace of Versailles has always been linked to the name of Louis XIV and his descendants Louis XV and Louis XVI. Nevertheless the château existed already before Louis XIV's will and its history did not stop after Louis XVI's departure and the French Revolution. A selection of the important dates on the history of the château, from its construction up to now has been gathered here.

1623 : Construction of a Hunting Lodge, where Louis XIII enjoyed spending time. The Lodge contained an apartment for the King and about fifteen rooms for the guests as well as the necessary rooms for the service.

April 18, 1651 : Louis XIV's first visit in Versailles to hunt. He is twelve years old.

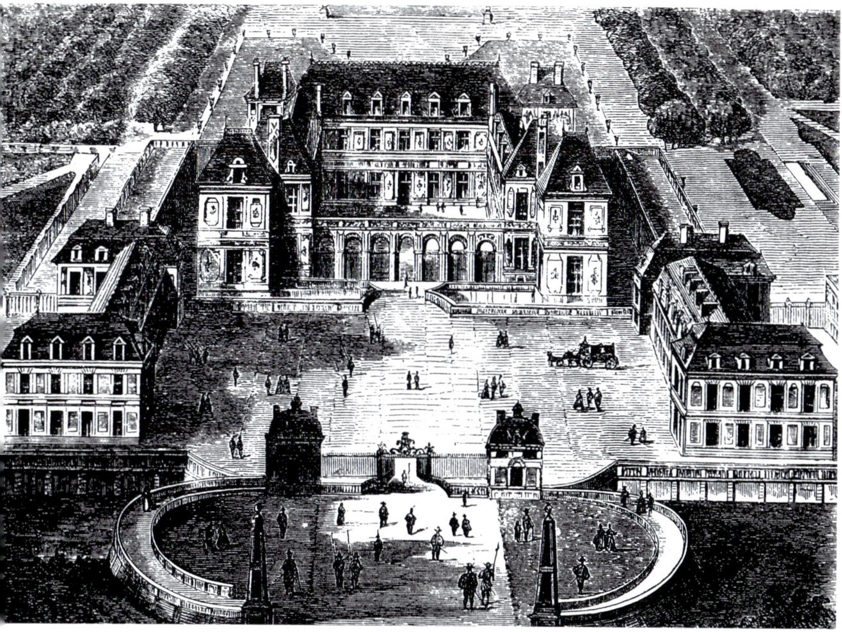

Versailles under Louis XIII

1654 : Louis XIV is crowned.

1661 : Beginning of Louis XIV's reign.

August 17, 1661 : King Louis XIV is invited by Nicolas Fouquet, then Superintendent of Finances, to celebrate the achievement of his own cast-

The palace of Vaux le Vicomte

Fouquet

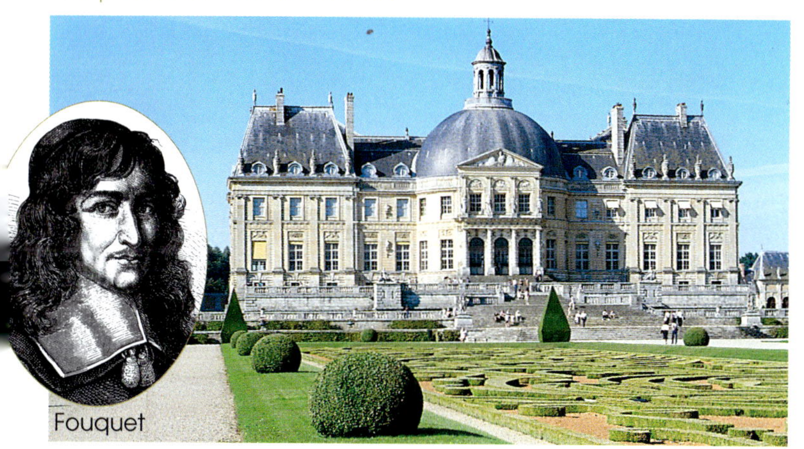

le in Vaux-le-Vicomte. 6 000 people are invited to the celebration, whose splendour produces the King's jealousy. Fouquet is arrested in September 5th, by d'Artagnan, and is jailed in the Pignerole fortress. Fouquet's decorators, gardeners, architects, writers… and even his orange trees are picked up by the King. Fouquet is

Mademoiselle de La Vallière

Madame de Montespan

Louis XIV painted by Rigaud

then replaced by Jean-Baptiste Colbert in his functions next to the King.

June 1662 : Beginning of the work directed by the architect Louis Le Vau. The development of the gardens are confided to André Le Nôtre and the inside decoration to Charles Lebrun.

1663 : Le Vau starts the construction of a first small orangery.

May 7th to 13th, 1664 : Celebration of the " plaisirs de l'île enchantée " (the pleasures of the enchanted isle). The genuine queen of the celebration is Louise de La Vallière, the King's favourite.

Lebrun

Didier Reuss

1667 : Digging of the Grand Canal.

1668 : Versailles diversions, organized to celebrate the first big campaign of work. Officially, these parties are due to the peace of Aachen, but they actually show the arrival of the King's new favourite, Madame de Montespan.

1671 : The Grand Canal is finished. Entertainments are organized on boats ; gondolas offered by the Doge of Venezia, models of galleys imagined by Colbert to make

The Grand Canal at the edge of the Royal Avenue

The marble courtyard

the King aware of the development of his naval fleet.

1672 : Construction of the Ambassadors' Staircase, a huge staircase leading to the King's apartment.

1673 : Louis XIV's illegitimate children are legitimated. They now have a rank halfway between princes of royal blood and dukes and peers.

1674 : A six days long celebration is given to Madame de Montespan, then at the height of her fame. Huge scandal : the lovers are both married. The embarrassing husband has been estranged by the King : Monsieur de Montespan slaps publicly his wife and orders to have horns on his coach so that to show everybody that his wife cuckolded him.

1678 -1684 : Construction of the Hall of Mirrors. 5 000 working hours were necessary for the making of each mirror. On the ceiling, Charles Le Brun imagined to relate the main episodes to the glory of the King.

1679 : Construction of the small and the great stables.... The great stables contain about 300 saddle horses whereas the small stables mainly house draught horses (about 800).

March 13, 1679 : Arrest of Catherine Monvoisin. The poisons scandal comes like a thunderbolt. Madame de Montespan is involved : she would have made the King drink potions and would have participated into black masses. This affair threw Madame de Montespan's fall.

1681 : Construction of the Marly engine, destined to bring water from the Seine River to Versailles. The supplying of the fountains of Versailles has always been

The great stables

Didier Reuss

problematical. When Louis XIV showed the garden round, the gates of the fountains were open step by step as he was walking, and then were closed just behind him.

1681 : The decoration of the King's State Apartments is achieved.

May 6, 1682 : The government settles in Versailles and the Palace becomes the King's main home. The King decides to abandon the constant movement of the Court, although it continued to go to other castles such as Fontainebleau or Compiègne every year.

1682 – 1684 : Construction of the Grand Lodgings. This is the " kitchen ", situated outside the castle so as to limit the risk of fire. The distance between the lodgings and the King's table was long and dishes were often cold when they arrived. They were then generally warmed-up on little stoves.

1683 : Achievement of the King's kitchen garden. Jean

The King's kitchen garden, created by La Quintinie

Baptiste de la Quitinie needed five years to turn the 9 hectares of marshy grounds into a place of production, experimentation and acclimatization of fruits and vegetables.

1683 : Death of Colbert. He is replaced in his functions by the Marquis de Louvois, his main opponent.

July 30, 1683 : Death of the Queen Marie-Thérèse of Austria in terrible sufferings. At

Colbert

the time, medicine hardly cured people when they had serious diseases. The Queen gave birth to 9 children, but only one would become adult.

Fall 1683 : The secret marriage between Louis XIV with Madame de Maintenon probably dates from this period.

1684 : Achievement of the Hall of Mirrors, and construction of a new wider orangery by Mansart.

Louvois

Madame de Maintenon

August 1684 : Louis XIV takes the decision to divert the water of the Eure River to supply the fountains of the park. So as to face the huge expenses engendered by the war of the League of Augsburg, he will quickly give up this idea.

May 15, 1685 : The Doge of Genoa comes to humble himself before Louis XIV and apologizes for his support toward the Spanish cause.

October 18, 1685 : Revocation of the Edict of Nantes, which offered the Protestants freedom of worship. Protestants are forbidden to practise their religion any longer. They are not allowed to leave the country either. Nevertheless, thousands of them will succeed in leaving France.

November 18, 1686 : The King is operated for an anal fistula. The King's surgeon, Felix, first trained in operating poor people, used as " guinea-pigs ", suffering from the

The Grand Trianon

The Grand Trianon

same disease. Some of them did not come through. The King kept it secret until the operation was made successfully. He made his best to hide his pain and not to change any of his daily occupations.

January 22, 1688 : Inauguration of the new castle of Trianon, built to replace the old dilapidated porcelain Trianon. The name " Trianon " comes from a village incorporated into the domain by the King, and eventually destroyed and replaced by a little decorative pavilion, covered with white and blue porcelain.

1688-1697 : The work of Versailles slowed down by the war against the League of Augsburg.

November 2, 1689 : So as to cover the cost of the war driven by the King, the silver pieces of furniture (throne, candelabras, girandoles...) of his apartment have to be melted down. The aristocracy is compelled to participate to the effort (i.e. delivering silver dishes...).

1692 : Louis XIV tries to place his illegitimate children. He imposes his nephew, the Duke of Chartres (son of his brother, the future regent) to marry one of the daughters he had with Madame de Montespan. Madame, mother of the Duke of Chartres, learning that her son accepted this misalliance, slaps him in front of the whole Court.

Charles II

November 1700 : Death of Carlos II, King of Spain. Carlos II not having any direct heir, Louis XIV's grand son, the Duke d'Anjou, was designed as successor in his testament. European powers soon rose up against this risk of hegemony. This event is the beginning of the war of Spanish Succession.

The grand Trianon

The Grand Trianon

1701 : In Versailles, the King settles in his new bedchamber, situated in the middle of the castle. From his windows, he can watch the whole town, whose constructions are strictly limited in height. The bedchamber is positioned facing east. The King thus benefits the sun rise. This bedchamber is a primordial room, where daily ceremonies of the King's rising and retiring take place.

The castle viewed from the marble courtyard

Inside the royal Chapel

January, February 1709 : Thousands of people die because of the winter cold. In Versailles, it is said that wine froze in the glasses, birds fell down while flying and some people were found dead in front of their fireplaces. The great misery of the population worsened this year because of the consequences of the war of Spanish Succession.

1710 : Achievement of the royal Chapel after 11 years of work. Unlike what occurred in the Palace of the King of Spain, the Escorial that was built around a chapel, the King hesitated a long time before he decided a definiti- ve place for his chapel.

The royal chapel from the main courtyard

February 15, 1710 : Birth of future King Louis XV.

17th Century

Pierre Corneille
(Rouen 1606 - Paris 1684)

Jean de La Fontaine
(Château-Thierry 1621 - Paris 1695)

The Temple of Love in the gardens of Trianon

Didier Reuss

great French writers

Molière (Jean-Baptiste Poquelin)
(Paris 1622 - Paris 1673)

Madame de Sévigné
(Marie de Rabutin-Chantal)
(Paris 1626 - Grignan 1696)

Nicolas Boileau
(Paris 1636 - Paris 1711)

Jean Racine
(La Ferté-Milon 1639 - Paris 1699)

1711 : Death of the Dauphin (smallpox), Louis XIV's son and heir to the throne. This date is the beginning of a huge hecatomb amongst the heirs of the Crown of France. The Duke of Burgundy, victim of treatments of the Court doctors. This child, who is Louis XIV's grand son, miraculously cured, will later become King Louis XV.

measles, is buried with his father in February 1712. The two children of the Duke of Burgundy also soon suffer from the same disease. The elder son dies, too. Only the youngest will survive, thanks to the devotion of the Duchess of Ventadour, his governess, who succeeded in putting him out of the hazardous

1713 : The Peace of Utrecht is signed, putting an end to the war of Spanish Succession.

July 1714 : Legitimated Princes become princes of royal blood. Through this Act, they might even reach the Throne. This decision provokes a general indignation.

In the park. Children with a bird - Simon Mazière

September 1, 1715 : Death of Louis XIV. The Court leaves Versailles. Louis XV settles in Vincennes where the climate is judged better for him.

1717 : Visit of Peter the Great (of Russia) in Versailles.

June 15 1722 : Louis XV comes back and settles in Versailles.

December 2, 1723 : Sudden death of the Regent Philippe of Orléans in his study room in Versailles.

On the left, Pierre Le Grand ; on the right, Philippe of Orléans

Marie Leszinska

September 5, 1725 : Marriage of Louis XV with Marie Leszinska. The King had been previously engaged to the infant of Spain, Marie Anne de Bourbon, born in 1718. Face to the urgency for the Throne of France to have an heir rapidly, the child, judged too young, is sent back to her country (this was followed by a huge diplomatic scandal). Then another fiancée, old enough to become pregnant, was chosen : Marie Leszinska who was then 23 years old.

August 14, 1727 : Birth of Louis XV's twin daughters. They are the first children of the royal couple. In 10 years, Marie Leszinska, gave birth to 10 children; 8 daughters and 2 sons. The daughters were surnamed Madame Première (Madame the First), Madame Seconde (Madame the Second), Madame Troisième... Most of them will remain unmarried, because of the lack of pretenders having their rank. They will eventually be sent to the Fontevrault abbey where they'll receive their education.

Statute of (young) Louis XV

September 4,1729 : Birth of the Dauphin in public (fear of a substitution of infants). 120 gun shots are fired : the bells of the churches are ringing for two days to celebrate the event. (The name " Dauphin " originally comes from the uniting of a region called Dauphiné (eastern France) to France. The King thus took an oath to name his elder son " Dauphin ").

1738 : Louis XV converts a part of the castle into a private apartment : the great ceremonial bed chamber where Louis XIV was dead is no longer used, except for the ceremony of the King's rising and retiring. In reality, the King sleeps in a smaller bed chamber, which, besides, is much easier to warm.

February 8, 1747 : Second marriage of the Dauphin, Louis XV's son, with Marie Josèphe de Saxe. Three sons

of this couple will be crowned later. The first is Louis XVI, the second, known as Count of Provence before the French Revolution will become Louis XVIII with the Restoration. After the death of Louis XVIII, the Count of Artois, then taking the name of Charles X, will ascend the Throne.

1752 : Destruction of the Ambassadors' Staircase. This huge staircase was covered with a wall of glass, whose waterproof ness was not properly made. The decoration thus quickly damaged.

The Count of Artois

The Petit Trianon

January 5, 1757 : Louis XV's assassination attempt by Damiens. While leaving the guards room to get into a coach that should drive him to Trianon, the King is violently jostled. The King first thought he was struck by a punch and then realized he had been stabbed. Fortunately the wound was not serious. Damiens will be quartered and will dead in terrible sufferings.

1764 : Delivery of the Petit Trianon, after two years of work. Built by Jacques Ange Gabriel, originally ordered by the King for Madame de Pompadour, the Petit Trianon will be offered later by Louis XVI to Marie Antoinette.

Louis XVI's and Marie-Antoinette's mausoleum in Saint-Denis

Madame du Barry

April 15, 1766 : Death of the Marquise de Pompadour, born as Jeanne Antoinette Poisson. Her reign had begun 21 years sooner. The King's favourite is dead in the Palace of Versailles. Her body is discreetly taken away to another place, under the King's eye who attempts her departure from the window of his study (in theory, only Kings and their families are allowed to die inside the castle.)

May 15, 1768 : Signature of the Treaty of Versailles with the Republic of Genoa. France accepts to pay the debts of the Republic, and receives in exchange Corsica as compensation.

April 1769 : Presentation of Madame du Barry to the Court. The favourite can thus officially go around with the King, and she is no longer obliged to go back to her hotel in the morning. The Court is chocked by this new favourite, of low birth and whose origins are doubtful.

May 16, 1770 : Inauguration of the Royal Opera for the marriage of the Dauphin, future Louis XVI and Marie Antoinette. An ingenious system allowed raising the floor on the same height as the stage. It was thus easily possible to turn the exhibition hall into a dance hall.

May 10, 1774 : Louis XV dies of smallpox. As soon as the death is certified, a candle is blown out and the courtiers rush towards the apartments of the new sovereign, Louis XVI, in order to salute him. The illness having caused the death of the King being infectious, his body is taken to the Saint Denis abbey, necropolis of the Kings of France

Saint Denis Basilica where Kings of France then used to be buried, with a ceremony reduced to a minimum.

June 5, 1775 : Coronation of Louis XVI.

1778 : Construction of the Temple of Love and the Belvedere.

La Fayette, one of the architects of the American independence with his friend George Washington

The farmhouse of the queen's hamlet

September 3, 1783 : End of the American war of independence. Benjamin Franklin had come to ask for the support of Louis XVI and of France, and

a treaty of trade and alliance had been signed in February 1778.

1783-85 : Construction of the Queen's Hamlet.

June 23, 1784 : François Pilâtre du Rozier performs a flight for the Court in his " Marie-Antoinette " Montgolfier.

August 15,1785 : Public arrest of the Cardinal de Rohan in the castle. Queen Marie Antoinette's necklace affair breaks out. The Cardinal de Rohan let himself convince to buy on credit a diamonds

necklace for the Queen.
He delivered it to a so-called intermediary who disappeared with the necklace. The jewellers asked directly to the Queen for a payment that was long to come. The Queen was completely taken aback. The inquiry that followed and the suspicion climate that surrounded this affair stained even deeper the monarchy.

1787 : Delivery of the Queen's Hamlet, whose work had begun in 1783 under the direction of the architect Richard Mique.

Louis XVII

May 5, 1789 : Opening of the General States at the " hôtel des Menus Plaisirs ".

Nymph with a pitcher and a horn of plenty - Jean Raon

June 4, 1789 : Death of Louis XVI's elder son. His brother (future Louis XVII) then becomes Dauphin.

July 14, 1789 : After the storming of the Bastille, many aristocrats are scared. A first wave of immigration follows quickly, including for instance the brothers of King Louis XVI (the future Kings Louis XVIII and Charles X). Versailles partly empties from this time onward.

October 6, 1789 : Louis XVI definitively leaves Versailles for the Tuileries Palace in Paris.

June 22, 1791 : After the fight to Varennes : the King had attempted to fly away. He was arrested in Varennes near Metz and brought back to Paris. Seals were put on the Palace by the municipality.

September 11, 1792 : A deputy asks for the casting of the statutes of the groves and fountains so as to make ammunitions.

January 21th, 1793 : Louis XVI is beheaded on the "place de la Révolution" (wich is nowadays "place de la Concorde).

June 10, 1793 to August 11, 1794 : Dispersion of the royal pieces of furniture, divided up into 17 000 shares. The most outstanding pieces are stored to be shown into the Louvre museum, then in project.

July 8, 1793 : A decision to create into the Palace a "mental school for the Republicans ". Yet, the castle is used as a mere storehouse for the revolutionary seizures of " Seine et Oise " (area south west of Paris).

October 16th, 1793 : Queen Marie-Antoinette is executed.

1794 – 1796 : The Grand Canal is destroyed and the ground is drained. Orchards are created on the south and north Parterres of the castle.

The hall of mirrors

The river Rhone, by Jean Baptiste Tuby

1795 : An inn is installed on the Petit Trianon, and a ballroom nearby, in the gardens.

1804 : Versailles is registered on the list of Napoleon's imperial residences. The latter mainly intervenes in restoring and refurnishing the Grand Trianon.

Louis XVIII

Louis-Philippe 1st

The fountain of Flora (or spring), by Tuby

1814 : All the apartments of the castle are repaired by Louis XVIII.

1833 : Louis-Philippe decides to turn Versailles into a museum, dedicated to " toutes les gloires de la France " (all the Glories of France) : huge work, several apartments are then demolished. 6 000 paintings are gathered, either coming from existing collections or especially executed for this project. The museum will be inaugurated four years later.

Napoléon 1st

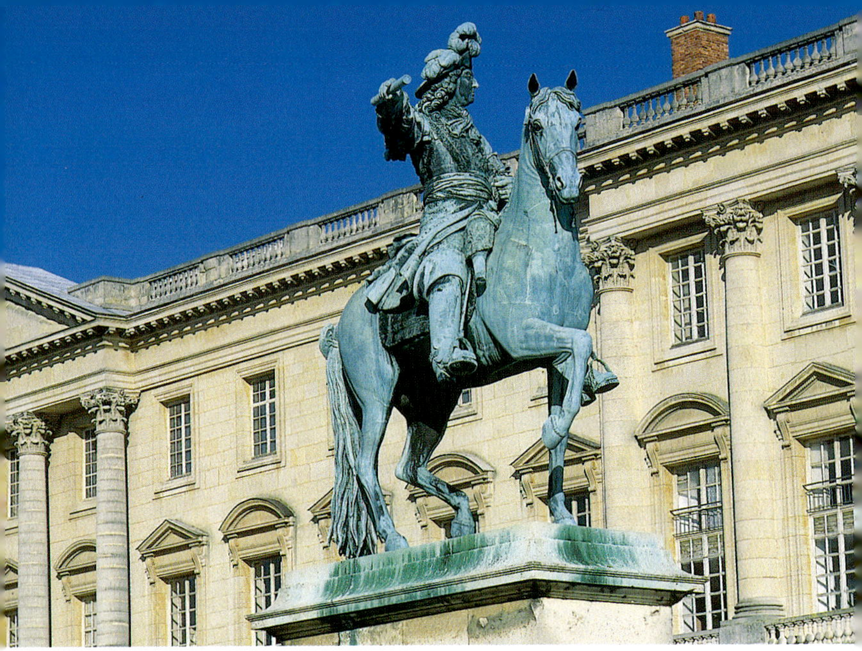

Louis XIV's statute, in the midle of the main courtyard

1836 : The Statute of Louis XIV on his horse is laid down in the middle of the main courtyard of the Palace of Versailles. The statute is due to Catellier and Petitot.

Victoria, Queen of England

1837 : Inauguration of the Museum of Versailles by Louis Philippe.

August 25, 1855 : Visit of Queen Victoria in the Palace of Versailles. The very first photographs known from Versailles were taken on this occasion.

August 3, 1862 : First " fêtes de nuit " for outside visitors.

January 18, 1871 : Shortly after the Sedan defeat, which hastened Napoleon III's fall, William 1st, King of Prussia, proclaims himself First German

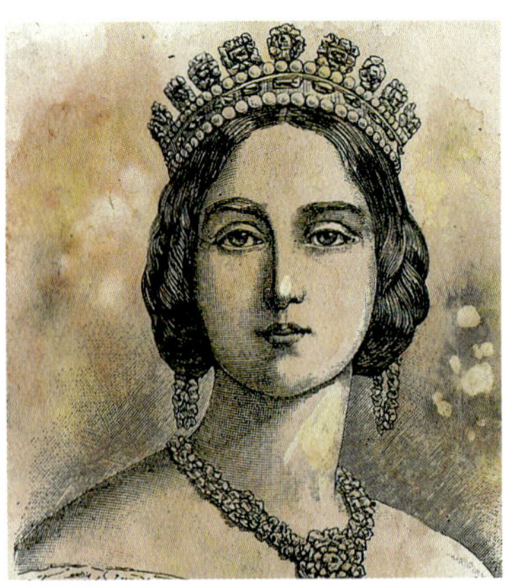

The back wall of the palace is a masterpiece of classical art

The fountain of Saturn, by Girardon, symbolizing winter.
This pictures
shows the vegetation of the gardens before the storm of 1999

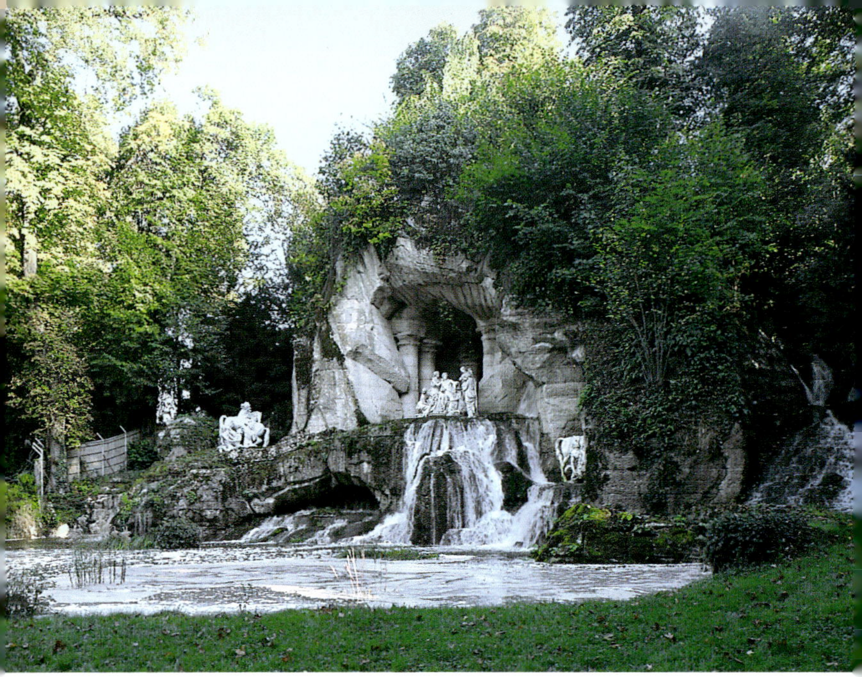

The grove of the Baths of Apollo

Emperor inside the Hall of Mirrors.

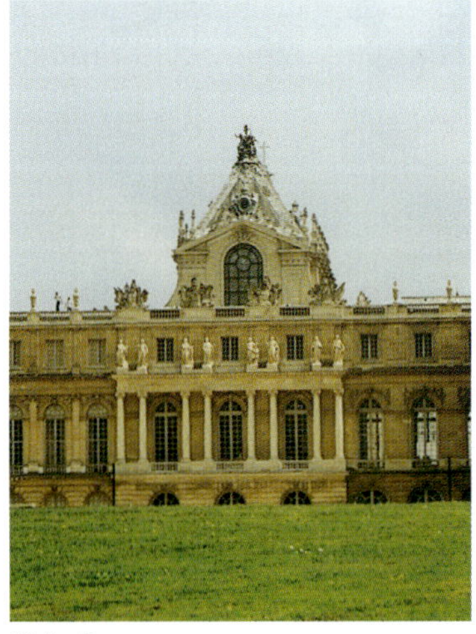

1871 : The Opera is transformed into a Session Hall for the National Assembly. It will be restored into its original state from 1952 to 1956.

August 10, 1901 : Two English women claim they have met the ghosts of persons who used to spend time in the Trianon during the 18th Century. They tell their adventure in a book that will enjoy a tremendous success.

June 25, 1907 : Birth of the " Société des Amis de Versailles " (Society of the Friends of

The royal Chapel, from the gardens

Didier Reuss

Versailles), which actively helps to restore and to refurnish the castle.

June 28, 1919 : Signature into the Hall of Mirrors of the Treaty of Versailles, that officially puts an end to the First World War. It is still possible to see the desk on which the treaty was signed in the private cabinet of Louis XV's apartment.

1923 : John D. Rockefeller makes a first settlement to finance the rehabilitation of the roof of the Palace of Versailles, the Petit Trianon, the Queen's Hamlet, the fountains and the sculptures of the park (other settlements will be made in 1927 and 1932). Still today, an important part of the work in refurnishing the rooms and in restoring the Palace of Versailles come from private founds (private persons as well as miscellaneous big companies).

1924 : Restoration of the Grand Trianon, the Queen's Theatre and the Queens's Hamlet thanks to the Rockfeller settlement.

Entrance by the main courtyard

Electricity has to be urgently installed for the occasion.

1963-66 : Restoration of the Grand Trianon, yet destined to become a presidential residence. It is inaugurated in 1966.

1975 : The cloth that now decorates the Queen's bedchamber is replaced. The original pattern, representing a bunch of flowers and peacock feathers, had been realized for Marie Antoinette in 1787.

1952 –1956 : The Opera is the subject of a rehabilitation programme. Original colours have been rediscovered, but the mechanism allowing raising the ground is suppressed.

July 6 – September 6, 1953 : Shooting of Sacha Guitry's famous film " Si Versailles m'était conté " (If I were told Versailles).

1961 : Visit of the American President John Fitzgerald Kennedy in Versailles. A diner is given into the Hall of Mirrors.

1975-1980 : Campaign of restitution of the Hall of Mirrors, as it must have appeared in the eyes of visitors in 1770. The hall, now without any piece of furniture is redecorated with 24 candle sticks, 20 centre lights (8 big and 12 small), and several statutes are replaced.

June 26, 1978 : Bomb attack in the ground floor rooms, in the south wing. Independents of Brittany (a region in western France) claim the responsibility for the attack.

The fountains in the baths of Apollo

June 4, 1982 : Opening of the G 7 summit in the Palace of Versailles.

1984 : The architect Jean Dumont builds the monumental staircase, originally planed by Gabriel in 1772 in replacement of the Ambassadors staircase, and that has never been achieved because of lack of money.

June 21st and 22nd, 1988 : Concert of the English Rock band Pink Floyd place d'Arme, in front of the Palace of Versailles with an audience of more than one million people. In 1992, the French musician Jean-Michel Jarre also makes a show on the place d'Arme.

February 2, 1990 : A storm provokes huge damages into the park of the castle. Beginning of a campaign of replanting the trees in the park.

December 26, 1999 : A violent storm blows more than 10 000 trees down into the park of Versailles. The replanting programme is increased.

The fountains of Neptune

General view of the palace

The palace from the Royal Avenue

Versailles in a few figures...

1. The Buildings

The Castle.

Under Louis XIII, the castle is mainly a house dedicated to the hunting pleasures that grew during the successive reigns of the Kings of France. During the nineteenth Century, when the Castle was turned into a museum by Louis Philippe, many elements disappeared.

Area of the castle : 11 hectares.

Length of the back side : 570 metres.

Roofs represent a total area of 120 000 m2.

Surface of the domain : 1 064 hectares.

The highest point of the Palace is the chapel cross, situated 46 meters above the main gateway (134.29 metres above the sea level).

Nowadays, the castle is composed of 700 rooms. There were 1 300 rooms at the time of the Revolution, in 1789. At the end of the 1680 years, the castle was constituted of about 1 840 rooms on the same level, and of 810 entresol rooms.

2 143 windows.

Besides, some of the rooms were heated with hot-air vents (a central heating system). The number of fireplaces was reduced when Louis Philippe turned the palace into a museum, and today only 352 remain.

In 1756, we could make an inventory of 226 apartments,

Didier Reuss

The Hall of Battles

68 staircases.

In 1781, there were 1 252 fireplaces.

to which those of the royal family have to be added. There were 188 apartments in 1781.

The main halls

The Hall of Mirrors is made of 17 arches of 21 mirrors each, thus a total of 357 mirrors. The hall is 70 meters long, 12.5 high and 10.2 wide.

The Hall of Battles, that welcomes 33 huge military paintings ordered by Louis Philippe, is 120 meters long and 13 meters wide.

The ceiling of the Hercules room measures 315 m2. The painter François Lemoyne needed 3 years to achieve it. The Hercules room measures 275.89 m2 (19.32 x 14.28). The difference is due to the fact that the ceiling is vaulted.

The Chapel stretches over 728,28 m2 (39,14 x 20,13).

The Crusades room occupies 262,25 m2 (23,28 x 11,28).

Buildings and outbuildings

The Orangery measures 6 140 m2. The main central gallery is 155 meters long and 12 meters wide. The height under the vault is 13 meters. Under Louis XIV, the orangery sheltered 1 080 trees : orange trees, bay-trees, olive trees, pomegranate trees. Nowadays, the orangery shelters 1 350 plants of which 850 orange trees.

The 103 steps of the famous staircase,
on the western side of the orangery

The two staircases that surround the Orangery are called the " Hundred Steps ". They actually have 103 steps on the west and 104 on the east.

The Place d'Arme (in front of the castle, nowadays a parking lot) measures 8.48 hectares.

The Diana Drawing Room
The entrance of the Hall of Mirrors, from the salon of War

The salon of War

Great Stables (former area) : 5 hectares. They sheltered the King's saddle horses (about 300 in the 17th Century).

Grand Lodgings : 0.64 hectares (originally the old kitchens of the castle, then later turned into a military hospital and recently returned to the domain of Versailles.)

Grand Trianon : the building measures 0.46 hectares.

Petit Trianon : 0.06 hectares.

Salle du Jeu de Paume (Tennis Court Oath Hall) : 32.82 x11.82 (a place where people used to play an old game called " jeu de paume " that could be compared to tennis. This hall, chosen for the famous " Tennis Court Oath ", is now a part of the domain.)

The Mercury room, also called the State bedchamber. It used to be th
ceremonial chamber of the big State Apartments

2. Gardens and fountains

The progressive purchase of the land and the villages under the reign of Louis XIV allowed the King to constitute step by step a huge hunting domain. It is said that in 13 years, Louis XIV would have killed 189 254 game animals or game birds !

Before the Revolution, the domain spread out on 8 000 hectares. At the time, a 43 kilometres long wall surrounded the whole domain.

815 hectares : surface of the domain of Versailles today.

700 metres : length of the Pound of the Swiss. The Pound of the Swiss spreads out on 20 hectares, the lake itself occupies 12.67 hectares.

1 600 metres : length of the Grand Canal. The water of the Grand Canal spreads out on 23.13 hectares. You have to walk 5 500 metres to turn around the Canal. The 500 000 m3 of earth had to be

removed for the digging of the Grand Canal.

The King's Garden, created in 1818 under the reign of Louis XVIII constitutes an untypical vegetal unity. This English garden also needs constant care. On 2 hectares, you can find 25 000 flowers and 3 000 trees.

The parks and gardens of Trianon develop on 95.11 hectares.

Every year, about 15 000 floral plants are produced by the gardeners of the domain so as to decorate the park.

The King's kitchen garden, which used to furnish the King's table on fruits and vegetables represents 9.48 hectares.

The sculptures of the little park contain 23 bronze subjects, 177 marble subjects, 253 marble basins, which makes a total of 453 sculptures.

The pound of the Swiss, beyond the orangery

The great organ in the Royal Chapel of Versailles

Nowadays, the park is composed of " only " 607 fountains. There were 1 400 fountains at the time of the Ancien Régime.

water consumption, 295 000 m3 of water in the Grand Canal, 12 000 m3 to play the show of the fountains. Most of the network dates from the time of Louis XIV.

Musical fountains :

A few figures : 32 basins, 50 fountains, 1 200 sprays (99 for the Fountain of Neptune), more than a thousand of hydraulic effects. 35 km of canalization, 3 600 m3/hour of

Today, the musical fountains take place about 45 times a year, on weekend and bank holidays. They attract more or less 540 000 visitors every year (in 2001 there were 548 879 visitors, which makes an average of 12 197 people a day.)

The fountains at the Colonnade

The fountains consume 62 000 hectolitres/hour.

Versailles every day

Versailles was a permanent building site (and to some extent it is still so !)... The construction cost of the Palace and domain is evaluated to 80 million Pounds. As a comparison, the State annual budget when Colbert was a

The Petit Trianon, built for Madame de Pompadour,
then offered to Marie-Antoinette

Minister was about 60 millions.

3 000 : Number of people housed in the castle or its nearby outbuildings at the time of the Ancien Régime.

10 000 : Number of people present in the castle during festivities. Usually, there were between 4 000 and 5 000 people

Daily life past

43 : Number of baths taken by Louis XIV in 26 years.

68 : Number of servants who assisted Louis XIV.

2.20 metres : height of the silver throne that was melted down in 1689 to help financing wars.

12 500 000 Pounds : price of the costume that Louis XIV wore when he received the Ambassador of Persia in February 19, 1715.

170 : The number of dresses ordered by Marie-Antoinette every year.

Today's castle

Frequenting : about 3 millions visitors every year
About 660 : number of workers employed by the establishment
To this, more or less one thousand seasonal workers every year have to be added.

In the gardens

Laocoon and his sons. Executed by Jean-Baptiste Tuby and
Jean Rousselet, finished in 1696

The statutes of the gardens deserve the most beautiful palace of the world
Faun playing flute - Simon Hurtrelle

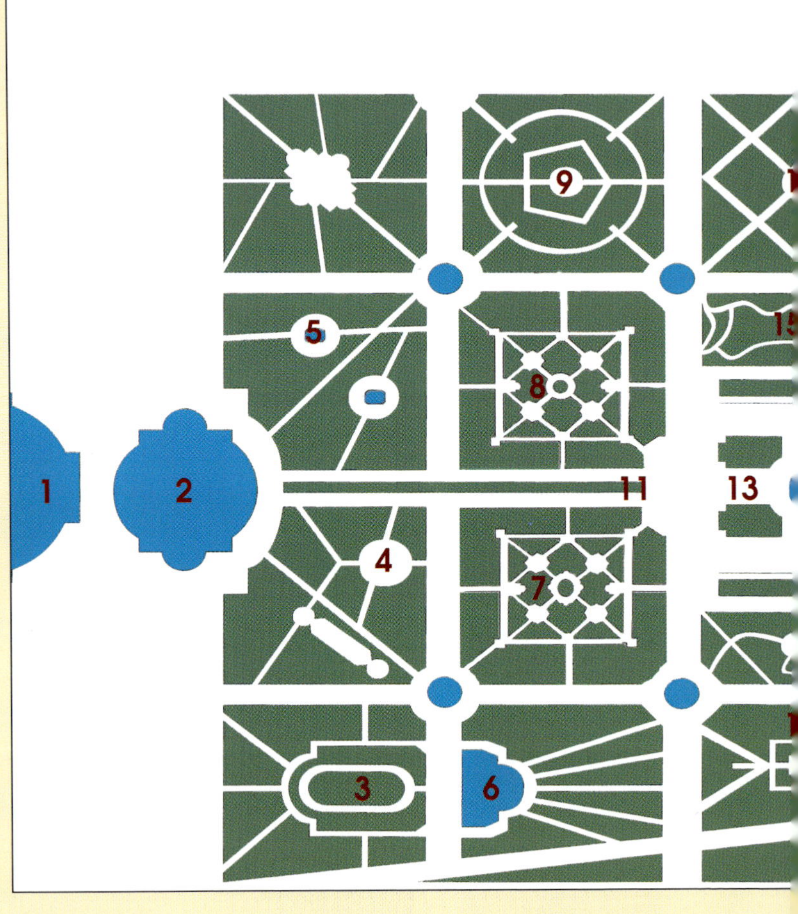

1- Grand Canal
2- Fountain of Apollo
3- King's Garden
4- Colonnade
5- Fountain of Enceladus
6- Water Mirror
7- South Quinconce
8- North Quinconce
9- Star Grove
10- Queen's Grove
11- Royal Avenue
12- Bosquet des Rocailles
13- Parterre of Latona
14- Fountain of Latona
15- Grove of the Baths of Apollo

Map of the gardens

Didier Reuss

Nymph with a shell
(copy of an ancient statute by
Coysevox, copied again by
Auguste Suchetet in the 19th
Century)

16- Rond vert
17- Parterre of the Orangery
18- Orangery
19 – 20 The Hundred Steps
21- South Parterre
22- Terrace
23- Water Parterre
24- North Parterre

25- Arc de Triomphe
26- Trois Fontaines
27- Dragon Fountain
28- Fountain of Neptune
29- Marble Courtyard
30- Louis XIV's Statute

Map of the Castle

1- Gabriel Pavilion	10- Coronation Room
2- Chapel	11- Hall of Battles
3- Crusades Room	12- Princes' Courtyard
4- Opera	13- King's Bedchamber
5- King's State Apartments	14- Dufour Pavilion
6- Salon of War	15- Marble Courtyard
7- Hall of Mirrors	16- Royal Courtyard
8- Salon of Peace	17- Louis XIV's statute
9- Queen's bedchamber	

© 2003 Editions Jean-Paul Gisserot
Imprimerie Pollina à Luçon N° L92620
Imprimé en France